Creative Acrylic
LANDSCAPES

Creative Acrylic LANDSCAPES

Wendy Jelbert

SEARCH PRESS

First published in Great Britain 2009

Search Press Limited
Wellwood, North Farm Road,
Tunbridge Wells, Kent TN2 3DR

Text copyright © Wendy Jelbert 2009

Photographs by Roddy Paine Photographic Studios

Photographs and design copyright © Search Press Ltd. 2009

ISBN 978-1-84448-171-2 4432 5800 8/10

The Publishers and author can accept no responsibility for any
consequences arising from the information, advice or instructions
given in this publication.

Suppliers
If you have difficulty in obtaining any of the materials and
equipment mentioned in this book, please visit the Search Press
website for details of suppliers: www.searchpress.com, or the
Winsor & Newton website:www.winsornewton.com for details of
your nearest Premier Art Centre.

Alternatively, please phone Winsor & Newton Customer Service on
020 8424 3253.

Publishers' note

All the step-by-step photographs in this book feature the
author, Wendy Jelbert, demonstrating how to paint with
acrylics. No models have been used.

There are references to sable and other animal hair brushes
in this book. It is the publishers' custom to recommend
synthetic materials as substitutes for animal products
wherever possible. There is now a large range of brushes
available made from artificial fibres, and they are satisfactory
substitutes for those made from natural fibres.

Printed in Malaysia

Acknowledgements

My thanks to Joss Newman and her computer for
helping so much! Also to my gorgeous children,
Rebecca, Richard, Rosalind, Claire and Emma, and my
patient and helpful husband, Paul.

Cover
Malvern Ridgeway
40.7 x 30.5cm (16 x 12in)

This painting also appears on page 95.

Page 1
Edge of the Cornfield
44.5 x 34.3cm (17½ x 13½in)

Pages 2–3
Summer Haze
40.6 x 30.5cm (16 x 12in)

This painting also appears on page 44.

Above
Varenna, Lake Como
28 x 38cm (11 x 15in)

Opposite
Scotland's Glow
37.5 x 31cm (14¾ x 12¼in)

CONTENTS

INTRODUCTION 6

MATERIALS 8

USING SKETCHBOOKS 12

USING PHOTOGRAPHS 14

LANDSCAPE SHAPES 16

TONE 18

COMPOSITION 20

BASIC TECHNIQUES 22

FOREGROUND AND DISTANCE 28

PAINTING SKIES 32

VARIATIONS ON A THEME 34

CONSTANTINE BAY 36

SUNFLOWERS 46

GOLDEN WOODLAND 56

COWS BY RIVER 66

LAKE GARDA 76

COLORADO FOREST 86

INDEX 96

INTRODUCTION

Throughout my teaching and painting career, experimenting and mastering the wide range of media available has been exciting and challenging, especially when I started to teach and had to pass on my knowledge to students. Acrylics were in their infancy as a medium then. The quality and range of colours quickly improved and I willingly used acrylics alongside my oils and watercolours.

I rapidly discovered that acrylics were the most versatile medium and I could easily incorporate many techniques and styles even in one work. Their 'oil' and 'watercolour', collage and glazing techniques are wonderful attributes for artists, both beginners and professional painters. Atmospheric wet into wet washes, the luscious, expressive application of buttery layers and the enhancing iridescence that gives mother-of-pearl effects are just a few impressive variations that you can capture in acrylics. Not only are there many techniques to master, but also several exciting additives that can be used with acrylics such as salt, food wrap, texture pastes and inks.

What are acrylics? They are a completely new type of paint for artists, the first for 300 years. They extend the painter's range, are clean to handle and have only a slight, pleasant aroma. Their speed of drying needs to be handled well – but this can be advantageous, as mistakes can be quickly altered. This quality is also a blessing when a single painting can develop from start to finish without interruption – you no longer need to wait for drying time. Even the thickest of paint can be varnished the same day.

Acrylics are made from polymer resin, and this binds with the pigments. Once dried, they cannot be re-wetted to lift or alter the colour. Until then, they may be manipulated like watercolours. Watercolours, which should be spontaneous and impressive, can become laboured, with the freshness quickly vanishing with overworking. Acrylics are adaptable and forgiving and seem to be the ideal solution to common problems associated with other media.

The adhesive quality of acrylic paints is excellent and they can be applied to any surface unless it is oil based, without leaking or peeling off.

This book explains how to apply acrylic paint and helps you to get to know its character and how it responds when used for various techniques. It is a magic that does not happen by itself, but the techniques explained here will help you to fulfil the potential of acrylics and, with plenty of practice, will enhance your ability to achieve successful pictures. This book concentrates on painting an assortment of landscapes covering coastal, mountains, lakes and traditional countryside scenes, and I hope these projects encourage you to explore the acrylics in all their guises. I will steer you through the sheer pleasure and versatility of painting in acrylics – and I am sure you will be hooked forever!

Opposite
Daisies and Thistles
34 x 45cm (13³/₈ x 17³/₄in)

6

MATERIALS

There are extensive ranges of acrylic paints, brushes, additives, knives and supports available. It is therefore well worth experimenting with several types to find out which suit you.

PAINTS

There are several starter kits with small tubes for those who wish to have a go, before committing themselves fully to one colour or one manufacturer. Try to buy the best paints you can afford, as the artists' quality are made from the finest pigments and have a better handling and richer texture than the cheaper students' alternative. There will be a difference between the brands when it comes to the drying time and the feel of the paint when you are applying it onto your chosen surface. Even within one manufacturer, there are thicker and buttery or runnier alternatives. Once you have opened a pot or tube, it is essential that the top is immediately replaced, or the paint will become dry and unusable.

Acrylic paints. It is important to select a palette before starting a painting, perhaps slightly adjusting if the subject requires. It is best to use only a few colours and intermix these to keep the painting cohesive. Too many colours result in a 'muddy' picture and lack of harmony within the overall effect. The colours I use are stated clearly at the start of each step-by-step demonstration.

BRUSHES

Again there is a wide and bewitching range available. You will need soft brushes made for watercolour, as well as harder, less flexible, hog-haired ones for the oil techniques. Never leave brushes in water for too long, as it damages them. After each session, they should be cleaned thoroughly with mild washing up liquid or soap.

Hog brushes: for the demonstrations in this book, I have used a no. 4 flat and a no. 2 filbert.

Watercolour brushes: I have used a 13mm (½in) flat, a no. 4 sable round, a no. 6 sable round and a rigger. These softer brushes are excellent for washes and areas that do not need the prominent brush strokes, but a more gentle and diffused area.

I do not use many smaller brushes as these can be too fussy and I often use old brushes, as these are handy for many effects such as foliage. I use the ends of the brushes again for scratching out techniques.

KNIVES

I use a variety of shapes in both metal and plastic. Painting knives have a raised handle and mixing knives are flat – although you can apply paint with either if needed. Knives can create luscious, thick and sumptuous effects with swathes of buttery paint – very expressive and fun to do! They are also ideal for applying texture pastes and gels.

From back to front: a painting knife, a 13mm (½in) flat, a no. 4 flat hog, a no. 2 filbert hog, a no. 6 sable round, a no. 4 sable round and a rigger.

PALETTES

There are several 'stay-wet' palettes on the market, especially designed for acrylics. I prefer these, as the home-made varieties made of freezer trays and food wrap tend to collapse and expose your paints so that they dry out and you lose them.

Tear-off palettes are useful for impasto and quick work, but these only work as long as the paint remains workable and have no capacity for keeping the paint damp.

PAINTING SURFACES

Acrylics can be applied to most prepared papers, canvases and boards. Avoid any surface that states it is for oil painting only, since acrylics will not adhere to these. I use different types of canvas and papers. There are special pads for acrylics, similar to watercolour ones. They are heavier to feel and can resemble a canvas finish. I often use these as well as normal 300gsm (140lb) Not surface watercolour papers.

When working in thicker paint, I apply the paint directly on to canvas or board or paper anchored down with tape on to a board. If preferred, you can treat the surfaces with a coating of white acrylic or primer first.

The step-by-step demonstrations in this book are all on 300gsm (140lb) Not watercolour paper; other illustrations are on the same or on canvas or prepared boards.

TEXTURE PASTES AND VARNISHES

The versatility of acrylics can be enhanced even further by the addition of texture pastes and gels. There is a wide range of these from different manufacturers. They contain added light or heavy sand, grit or fibres, used to create textural effects for things such as old walls, weathered steps and foliage.

I use a satin acrylic varnish after completing my work. A compromise can be obtained by using a half matt and half gloss mixture (varnish or medium).

A painting board, kitchen paper, water pot, masking fluid, ruling pen and pencil, masking tape and plastic food wrap, and (right) a hairdryer.

OTHER MATERIALS

A hairdryer is used to speed up the drying of either paint or texture paste.

Masking fluid and a **ruling pen** are used for protecting fine work under washes.

Drawing inks can be used to create a pen and wash style effect in a painting with acrylics. I used nut brown and canary yellow inks in the Golden Woodland project on pages 56–63.

Kitchen paper is used for moving excess paint, for dabbing out lighter areas or for cleaning up.

I use a **painting board** for securing my work or for stretching paper. The paper is attached to the board using **masking tape** or gummed paper.

A pencil is used for preliminary drawings.

Plastic food wrap is for creating textural effects.

A **water pot** is used for mixing washes and for cleaning brushes as you paint.

Drawing inks and a ruling pen.

USING SKETCHBOOKS

The ability to draw and record the essentials of a landscape is the foundation of your future paintings. The gathering of vital information in your sketchbook and your initial response to the atmosphere, tones and colours of a scene will bear fruit in your finished pictures. Sketching in the open air is really rewarding, as this develops your observation and drawing skills, and the more you do, the better you will become.

There are no hard and fast rules. I always carry a firm, covered sketchbook, so it will not bend when I am using it on location. Sketches can be in pencil or pen, or small watercolour studies. I also include a 3B or 4B pencil, eraser and if possible carry a comfortable fold-up stool with a back support in my sketching kit.

Sketchbooks come in all sizes, shapes and varieties of paper. My favourite consists of three different papers: 185gsm (90lb) and 300gsm (140lb) Not surface watercolour, plus a heavy cartridge – this is suitable for everything – painting and sketching in one book!

Sketches capture more 'feeling' than a photograph and seem to emphasise poignant features more readily. They can also be altered back in the studio – but don't modify too much, or the painting will not resemble the original idea. I also note down the time of day, where the scene is, the year and direction of the light.

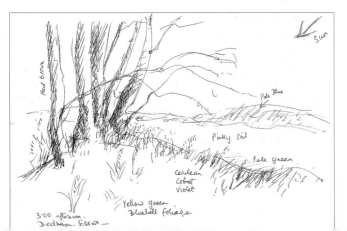

The bluebell painting (shown at the top of the page opposite) started as a quick pen sketch, backed up by a more detailed watercolour study of the wood leading up to the edge of the bluebell glade (see the pages in my sketchbook, above). I quickly realised this whole scene offered many options: it could easily be sub-divided, perhaps using the foreground on the left, or the central trees and flowers, or a portrait format of the right-hand side. I ended up choosing the section on the extreme right, of the trees overlooking the field, and I did a compositional sketch of this area (left) with colour notes.

Edge of Bluebell Wood

30 x 23.8cm (11¾ x 9³/sin)

The finished painting. I placed in an underpainting of burnt sienna which contrasted well with the vivid greens and the sunlit cerulean, cobalt and violet blues of the bluebells.

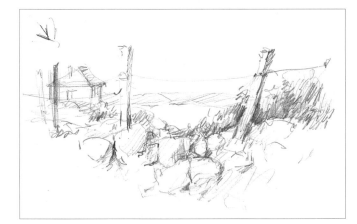

This quick pencil sketch has indications of distance, a house, and a textured foreground. In the finished painting (right), I moved the posts about and changed angles. I dropped the barbed wire, so the fields were viewed as a 'peephole' through the fence posts.

Using an outdoor sketch back in the studio has many advantages: the imaginative interpretation that can be achieved from one good, thoughtful sketch offers many alternatives and options for future work. You can change the colours or the season, or add atmosphere and mood to the picture, after experimenting more fully in your sketchbook. Sometimes this stage can take longer than painting the chosen picture! Once back in the studio, the weather conditions no longer contribute to the pressure to complete your work. You can take as long as you like now in getting a satisfactory result.

Cornish Stone Wall

40 x 28.2cm (15¾ x 11¹/sin)

I added the cow parsley in the studio using some of the textures mentioned on pages 26–27. Burnt sienna (neat) was painted under the stone wall to create a dramatic contrast to the greens in the distance and in the wall. Tonally, the cow parsley becomes light due to the dark paint behind the flower heads. The main features from the sketch were not compromised, but changed about a little to enhance the whole composition.

USING PHOTOGRAPHS

In our busy modern lives, taking photographs is sometimes the only way we have of gathering reference material when visiting a chosen place or landscape.

Photographs are an excellent form of detailed reference, and very valuable if used alongside a sketch, which hopefully emphasises a point not highlighted so dramatically in an over-detailed photograph. Photographs cannot, however, provide the spontaneity of the moment or the essence of why you liked the place. It is very tempting to copy other features from a photograph that were not in the first conception of the subject, so that everything becomes overwhelmingly fussy. This slavish copying of a photograph adds nothing but muddle. If possible, use photographs you have taken yourself, as you have a better understanding of the subject, and therefore may have the confidence to leave things out and keep everything simple.

There are some other pitfalls which can be overcome. Photographs can influence colour and tone, which tempts the artist to copy. Try out your own palette and see if you can improve on things. Try and take photographs in both full sunshine and duller weather if possible. The deep shadows are good for shapes, but you lose all details in their blackness. Duller weather produces more detail within the shadows. When accompanied by a preliminary sketch, some features such as a tree that seems to be growing out of a roof or someone's head, can be rectified, plus by sketching when photographing a more complex scene, you will understand how things work and what is happening within your subject.

When photography was first invented, artists used it to their advantage. Even some of the impressionists recorded scenes, and when used well, spontaneity and freshness are retained. The very fact that photography can record one kind of image, usually a very realistic one, seems to free some painters, who are encouraged to express themselves more personally and create an image that cannot be captured with a camera. If working from photographs helps, and you are aware of the pitfalls, if you are practising and creating more paintings, it is a good thing!

I have used photographs for a series of paintings of Pin Mill in Essex. This has been a famous spot for artists throughout the ages, and one I especially like is Edward Seago. I take a series of photographs, some depicting the scene from a distance, and from differing angles. I also try and capture the sea at low and high tides – this gives several options for additional pictures in the future.

Here the sea has exposed the textured stones and pebbles at low tide, and offered more reflections at a higher tide.

Here I have joined two photographs together, forming an elongated format. This gives a panoramic view of boats and the public house reflections. I waited for a small boat to appear, so this could be included as a good focal point, if required!

The final sketch of the scene before deciding to paint. This has notes about what I need to highlight in my work. I find that photographs for me are essential in compiling my sketches and I can use many reference photographs in only one painting.

COMBINING PHOTOGRAPHS

These are two photographs of a tree and landscape with a bridge and pathway leading into the picture. I thought that the trees around the bridge in the right-hand photograph were too similar and needed a contrast. I took the photograph on the left, of a feathery tree with a lovely shape, as well, and decided to use it to replace the shrubbery on the right of the other picture.

Autumn Landscape
40.7 x 30.5cm (16 x 12in)

This is a combination of the two photographs using a limited palette present in both reference materials – cerulean and cobalt blue, burnt sienna, cadmium yellow, violet and emerald green – plus white. An apricot coloured undercoat was added before painting, made from orange, white and cadmium yellow. This gives a unity throughout the picture where it is glimpsed through the following layers.

LANDSCAPE SHAPES

Artists need to be moved by a scene and in consequence have a compelling urge to paint it. The desire is very personal, but a successful picture contains a combination of exciting but simple shapes, atmosphere and emotional interpretation.

These shapes need to balance in every way and slot together like a beautifully designed jigsaw puzzle. The beauty of your landscape reveals communication through a fine thread of painting techniques, emotion and good composition. Unless you enjoy the early construction stages and can control your urges to add colour, until you have established the foundations and skeletal design of your subject, you will not fully enjoy the stages to come! We need to understand how abstract forms build up our compositions, each depending on one another.

Landscapes have been a tradition in painting for centuries, offering great variety and potential. We present-day painters have to capture the distinctive qualities of our chosen place in our own style, often quite quickly, and with concentration on just a few strong thrusts of natural and characterful lines, markings and shapes that evoke a feeling of completeness.

If you work directly from life, the elements are ready at hand, and specific shapes may dominate and therefore should be emphasised, making other shapes more subservient, or even obliterated. Some artists need to reappraise the sketches and images back at home. Some passages of the picture might be developed further, whilst others remain the same. There are no set rules, so go with your feelings.

These are examples of initial sketches in pencil or ink. They have been analysed to show how the composition of each one is heavily dependant on several main shapes (shown in red). Even at an embryonic stage, a balancing act is taking place in a picture. Usually there are four main shapes, with further shapes added later on (shown in blue).

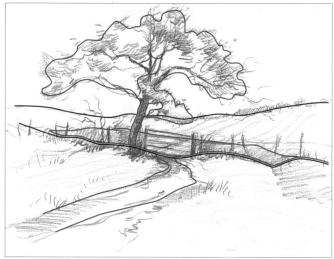

PUTTING SHAPES INTO PRACTICE

These acrylic colour sketches illustrate this principle.

The important emphasis is on the shapes of the river bank and the top of the tree, contrasted with the deep shadow shapes in the river.

The main shapes include the distant field and the folds in the foreground. Between these is the delightful, dark shape of the middle distant hedge, highlighting the two further fence posts.

The light swirl between the two main massed tree shapes and their shadows is vital to capture the essence of this picture. I placed this framework in first, followed by the larger and more complex shapes, leaving the centre light and open.

The light, domed shape of the distant field is well balanced with the larger sunlit foreground shape. This sandwiches the dark slither of shadow from the main tree. These ribbons of contrasting tone and colour often occur in landscapes and add vitality and drama to the scene.

TONE

Tone is how dark or light a subject is, irrespective of its colour. It can be confusing in a painting to recognise colours in terms of tone. A traditional way to discover the tonal quality of a scene is to screw up your eyes and look through your eyelashes so colour is diminished, and you can perceive the lights and darks more easily. Each colour has a tonal range, and seeing colour as tone is a skill that requires constant practice.

Tonal studies from my sketchbook.

Before painting, study the scene and see how the tones are distributed, the very darkest reserved for shadows and the lightest where the sun is most direct. The remaining will be a mixture of mid-tones linking both extremes of dark and light. The darkest area is the pivotal point, and no other part of the picture should be as dark. In a successful picture, all tones need to be judged correctly and pleasingly distributed – so a good picture will always reproduce well in black and white.

An excellent habit is always doing a small thumbnail tonal sketch of the scene before starting anything on the canvas or whatever surface you have chosen for the finished painting. Keep all areas simple, direct and with impact. At this vital stage, things can easily be changed about. I usually start the tonal sketch with the extreme lights and darks, where these contrasts form exciting patterns.

Traditionally, a painting in sepia or neutral tint was used to enhance a drawing, or used as an underpainting, with the colours placed over the top. The method has largely fallen out of favour with artists, some of whom now paint in a wide range of kaleidoscope colours, without understanding the tonal foundations that form a good solid picture! Remember that it is not the complication of a picture that counts, but the simple statements that deliver the most memorable results.

A sepia tonal study of St Mark's Square in Venice.

KEY POINTS

I limit my students to six tones. Of course there are many more, and these will become very obvious as you develop your understanding of tones. By playing about with the assorted tones, as in the exercise shown on the right, you may discover the versatility and excitement of how they work.

You can use watery blue and drop darks and lights together on a wet base and watch how they balance one another out.

A chart of five tones, or six if you count the first as white: then the next five are in different strengths of colour, with six being the darkest.

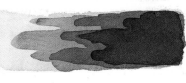

Try out different shapes and different strengths of blue. This gives a feeling of receding and perspective, essential in placing shapes for atmospheric effects.

Fading a dark tone into the most delicate shades exercises your ability to capture moods and climatic conditions.

For quick, dramatic and atmospheric results, I often use black Quink ink. When mixed with varying amounts of water, this forms unexpected and exciting tonal effects, with yellows and blues oozing out of the black ink. These 'doodles' give me a framework that I can then add to, enabling me to convey a vitality that I hadn't achieved in the traditional way.

This tonal pencil sketch was transferred into a painting using colour reference notes and tonal numbering and shading. If you have only a little time to complete the shading, you can use a numbering system instead, or as in this sketch, use both alongside each other.

CONTRASTS IN TONE

This technique uses contrasting shapes – lights against darks and vice versa – for dramatic and inspiring effects.

The bridge scene catches the light on the distant hillside, through the bridge archway, and across the right-hand bank. The dark tree highlights the lighter details of the bridge.

This scene shows the opposite effect, with the distant hill dark against the sunlit tree. The bridge reflection is also in the opposite tone.

The play of light on any scene will form a tonal relationship throughout the picture. The tones will offer information about the weather, time of day and mood of the moment. This will convey a deep communication of light and space and give a three-dimensional effect. Subtle tones can express calm and contrasts create a more dramatic and exciting scene.

COMPOSITION

Good composition is vital for a successful picture. No matter how well the artist has expressed colour and technique, if the underlying structure or composition is weak, then the whole exercise is lost!

Try not to 'say' too much, but present the subject matter so it is clearly understood. There should also be a sense of fun, excitement and the unexpected – something different for the viewer to discover and to give you a challenge.

CREATING A FOCAL POINT

This is your centre of interest and there should only be one per picture! Divide up your rectangle into thirds (as shown right) and this will form four intersecting points, where the perfect spot is created for a focal point. This place holds some vital information: the most details, the most colour and the most tonal contrast.

Do not divide your composition into halves, or place your focal point in the centre. Although it is good to have similar shapes in a picture, do not echo these too much, but vary their size for variety. It is best to have either one-third sky to two-thirds landscape or vice versa for the most satisfactory proportions.

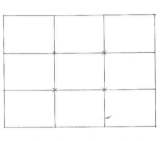

A landscape format divided into thirds.

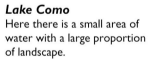

Lake Como
Here there is a small area of water with a large proportion of landscape.

River Reflections
This painting has two-thirds landscape with one-third sky.

20

BASIC DESIGN

Deciding what to include and exclude is essential in the early stages of a painting. My aim is usually to simplify the whole scene, and to do this I must decide, firstly, where my focal point lies. Next I decide on the basic blocks that build around this point – making them varied in colour and shapes. I need to allow some natural rhythm line to flow through the design, but to let some effects evolve and just happen, building and adapting as the picture proceeds.

Some compositions can be constructed on either a 'c', 'm' 's', 'v' or 'z' shape, for example, Lake Como opposite contains 'm' shapes, and River Reflections contains 'v' shapes. These shapes lead the eye around pathways through the scene. Some subjects need to be considerably exaggerated, whilst others should be understated, all depending on what you are trying to say in your picture.

I often take several photographs from different angles and try out several sketches, as this offers a wide range of options for future work. Sketches can be made in a variety of differing formats, as shown here.

This long horizontal sketch of Santorini, Greece, emphasises the panoramic feel of the early morning scene, with the buildings appearing to spread out over the island.

Santorini, Greece

48.3 x 35.5cm (19 x 14in)

The completed painting captures the awesome height of the mountainside with the whole town scattered and squatting over the magnificent site.

This elongated, vertical study captures the feeling of height as the buildings seem to cling to the mountainside.

BASIC TECHNIQUES

Painting in acrylics offers such a wide range of techniques. The paints are so versatile that they can be diluted and worked to give an appearance similar to that of watercolours. They can also be applied thickly to resemble oils.

The first pages will concentrate on the watercolour side of these paints. This diversity of application requires practice, and care should be taken to match the right method with your chosen subject.

WATERCOLOUR TECHNIQUES

Washes

These can be applied on a wetted or a dry surface.

For the flat or basic wash, mix enough colour before you start. With your largest brush, paint a horizontal stroke, recharge the brush and run it below, so that the two run together. Continue down the paper and, if any paint is left, apply paper tissues to the bottom edge to mop extra paint off.

Here I applied fairly neat colour first then gradually added more water as I worked down the paper, to create a graduated wash.

Blending

Blended washes such as these are ideal for landscapes and especially skies. They need lots of practice to master. They can be worked wet on a dry surface, or wet into wet.

Try two contrasting colours to start with. The wash on the left was worked on dry paper; the one on the right wet into wet.

Wet into wet

This technique also works well with multiple colours. Here I developed blues and yellows together into a wetted surface, and 'rocked' the image so the colours mixed into a green on the paper. A super abstract image to start a picture!

Using masking fluid

This is for creating highlights and intricate shapes. I use a ruling pen as an applicator, then apply a wash over the top. When the wash is dry, I remove the masking fluid to reveal the white patterns on the paper.

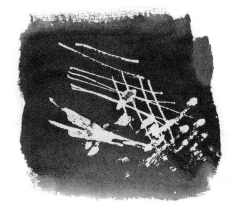

Glazing

When diluted with water, acrylics are translucent enough to allow one colour to be glazed over another, and full advantage can be taken of this by using the glazing technique in your work. It can alter or emphasise each colour as they cover one another. This is excellent for shadows or for adding a glow to your work. Here I have painted strips of blue, yellow, green and red and painted vertically across in similar colours on top.

Sponging

Fabulous effects can be created with sponges. Try out several kinds with various thicknesses of paint. Layers of sponged colours can add an alluring depth or a fragile but natural colouring to trees and shrubs.

Splattering

This is a technique that I use often to create random spots and specks of colour. I have wetted half of this example and applied an acrylic wash over it. To splatter paint, pick up the colour on your brush, push the bristles against your extended finger, then let them go. This is ideal for making walls look old and weathered, or for pebbled paths.

Scratching out

After a darkish colour has dried, fine or slightly broken lines can be scratched across the paint, exposing the original paper to create pale or white lines. You need to use a very sharp modelling knife and care should be taken not to cut right through your paper! You can also use the sharpened handle end of a brush. Scratching out can be used to rescue the lights needed in your work or to highlight features such as reeds or grasses.

If you scratch out when the painting has not dried, then the paint runs back into the small grooves and becomes darker. Sometimes, it drags to form blotches or blobs on the line. Either of these effects can be used in landscape painting, as they have a natural look.

OIL TECHNIQUES

As acrylics are so versatile, applying them on top of each other thickly and with expressive brush marks creates fabulously textured surfaces – so reminiscent of oil painting. Here we are exploring the ways you can capture some of these techniques.

Scumbling

I applied a neat base layer of blue on the paper. After drying, I used a painting knife and dragged a thick layer of yellow over parts to create blurred shapes with some of the original blue showing through.

Painting knives with thick paint

Acrylics can easily be applied to great effect with a painting knife – many shapes are available. Here I used colour straight from the tube, knifed it into an impasto and, with chopping and dabbing movements, formed some interesting strokes.

Dry brush marks

For these markings, excess water is taken from the brush. The paint can then be dragged and rubbed over the paper or canvas to impart open-weave textural effects, excellent for the edges of trees, foliage of all sorts, even, if using white on a dark background, for light glistening on a pond or sea. This technique works better if applied on a textured surface.

Different brush strokes

As with anything new, you need to discover how your brushes work when handling the paint. By experimenting, you will discover how much paint to apply, how much pressure to place on the brush for each marking, how to manipulate your elbow, wrist and the brush's tip to achieve a sweep or curling movement, or even a straight line. Time is needed for this important exercise. Try out dabs, dots, sweeps and many more. Also try out different colours and see how they seem to 'vibrate' and work together – a voyage of discovery is certainly ahead!

Scratching out

If an undercoat such as a deep blue is allowed to dry, other colours can be applied while it is still wet. Then, using a sharp instrument (the end of a knife blade, a brush handle or something similar), you can scratch through to the underlying colour. Even the original colour, while drying, could be scratched out, revealing a design through the thicker paint. These lines can be pronounced and textured and can produce a fascinating effect.

25

USING ADDITIVES

Acrylics have a limitless potential for the creation of all kinds of textures, which are both fun and challenging. There are many ready-made texture pastes and gels, but you can also use several materials from around the house such as sand, grit, eggshells, plastic food wrap and PVA glue to create other exciting effects.

These pages demonstrate the surface textures that can be achieved. Try these exercises out for yourself; you may discover other ways of expressing yourself in future work!

Many times, having conjured up a superb patterned surface, I have built up a painting around it, and it has proved to be a very successful first step in my picture making. The subject matter can also dictate a particular textural surface or theme. Try not to overload your picture with too much of one paste or too many varieties of texture in one go. Keep exploring these additives and soon you will create some marvellous results.

Texture pastes

There is a wide range of fabulous pastes and gels containing materials such as fibres, medium, fine and coarse grits and glass beads. Here I have tried out a smooth variety and a sandy type. Both are applied to the surface with a painting knife or hog hair brush and allowed to dry, then acrylic paints are applied over the top. They are excellent for aged and weathered walls and rocks.

Effects created using texture paste: smooth paste on the left and sandy paste on the right.

Salt

This can be very attractive and beguiling when used in a watercolour way with washy acrylics. Immediately sprinkle salt into the wash and then leave it to react chemically with the wetted paint. Ideal for sea effects, foliage and snowy atmospheric studies.

Effects created using salt in washes of acrylic paint.

Eggshells

After boiling an egg, peel off the shells ready for use. PVA glue can be used to secure the shells, which are excellent for creating the stone blocks of an old wall or, if broken up into tiny fragments, heads of cow parsley. You may need to weigh down the shells until dry with a jam jar filled with water. These collage textures can also include coloured papers, pencil shavings and even small pebbles, for painting over in acrylics.

Effects created using eggshells.

PVA glue

Swirling and dribbling PVA glue on the surface of your paper can create interesting effects. Leave it to dry or use a hairdryer to hurry things up, then cover the raised surface with acrylic wash. The colour will fall into the crevices and the lighter PVA glue pattern will protrude through the colour. This technique is ideal for watery movement in a painting such as swirling and splashing effects.

Effects created using PVA glue.

Plastic food wrap

Prepare a watery but colourful acrylic wash and then apply a creased piece of food wrap on to the surface so it captures air pockets and forms lovely patterns. Do not remove the food wrap until the paint is completely dry, otherwise the patterns created will be too weak and will slowly disappear. This technique is great for backgrounds, individual flowers, foregrounds and leaves and many other types of textured surface.

Effects created using plastic food wrap.

FOREGROUND & DISTANCE

As painters, we need to create a sense of depth: an illusion of a three-dimensional space. We also need to create a convincing foreground, middle ground and distance. This is quite a demand, especially when you are a beginner, but there are several ways of achieving it. Only one part of the painting should be emphasised and this should contain the focal point, whilst the remainder stays understated. Adding a recognisable object, such as a human being or animal, can help create an understandable scale to the whole scene. Including different shapes in warm colours, which appear to come forwards, or cool colours, which appear to recede, will considerably influence the look of the foreground and distance.

We have to invent a landscape to make objects appear three-dimensional and this will include shadows and shading as well as cool and warm colours. Very strong shading or exaggerated colours enhance their importance.

THE FOREGROUND – CREATING PERSPECTIVE

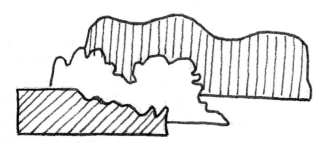

Here are the three recognisable spaces: foreground, middle ground and distance. Whatever the plane you have chosen to emphasise, the focal point needs to be included there. For the foreground, we need to create a feeling of a close-up, perhaps with glimpses of the remaining planes showing through. This creates a feel of scale immediately, and, coupled with brighter and more intense colours, makes an ideal picture.

Here I illustrate how I have worked out the rudiments of a painting from a sketch and a photograph. This photograph (right) of a rustic bridge with its structure highly exaggerated from a low angle, forms an interesting foreground.

As you will see in the sketch below, I always place an arrow sign to remind me where the sunlight is directed and this helps me to create correct shadows. I have changed the wooden structure slightly and the distant fence posts to achieve a more interesting lead-in that points towards the foreground. The darkened distant foliage helps to highlight the lighter wooden bridge in the foreground.

In this second example, the photograph (right) rather separates the foreground from the distance, and it needed more bonding of these two planes. The lovely composition needed exaggerating and highlighting.

In the preliminary sketch, (below, right) I corrected these two main problems. The flower close-ups helped push the mid-ground tree into the distance, but keeping it fairly dark helped to highlight the white front flowers. I still included the deep furrowed field on the left, as it contrasted well with the soft flowers and was an ideal lead-in line to the main composition.

The samples of foreground paintings below show how effective relatively simple objects can become, by grabbing our interest in the close-up zone. Partly revealing glimpses of the other planes helps to enhance the remainder of the picture.

Winter Field

25.4 x 17.8cm (10 x 7in)

The silhouette of the foreground broken fence is simple but dramatic, accompanied by the delicate, simple blue shapes of the distance.

Spanish Mountain Village

40.6 x 30.5cm (16 x 12in)

This scene was painted on the spot during one of my art courses. It was so magnificent: the village clinging to the cliff edge, snuggling between the vast and varied mountain shapes. The foreground oleander flowers heightened the feeling of depth by exaggerating the vast distance through their close-up details.

Gulls and Dunes

35.5 x 25.4cm (14 x 10in)

The darker grasses in the middle distance are essential for highlighting this foreground scattering of seagulls. Their counterchange of tone adds to the drama and action of the seascape. Their perceived size also gives an essential indication of scale.

THE DISTANCE

Within the following examples, we will soon discover that although the painting is divided into three sections (see the line drawing on page 28), distances can hold the focal point and break the rules by not becoming the usual faded blue space, but a dramatic and important section.

The foreground will now become subordinate and slightly muted, as in the photograph (right) of the ploughed field. This field just called out to be tamed and place in a picture! Those ploughed lines raced into the distance. I felt I had to place something of interest for my focal point, and use the other set of lines to play the other way and enhance the composition even more.

Moments before I took the photograph, a tractor disappeared into the distance. I reintroduced it, a dark and strong shape accompanied by swirling seagulls. This was in pencil, pen and ballpoint pen for the selection of tones I needed. A darker tone in the background helped with the action in the picture.

Following the Plough

51 x 40.6cm (20 x 16in)

The finished painting. I became fascinated by the tractor and flashing wings, and the way the furrows became important accents in the fabric of the picture. The focal point in the dark tractor is emphasised by the light fragments of active seagulls' wings. The cool shapes of the blue-coloured seagulls are now in the foreground. In the distance, burnt sienna and yellow ochre are dominant, warm shapes in the rich soil around the tractor.

This photograph and sketch show the glorious English planes, undulating and sweeping into a hazy distance. The accents of the trees and shrubs emphasise the atmosphere of wide open spaces, gently patterned by individual fields.

Lavender Field

35.5 x 44.5cm (14 x 17½in)

Here I painted purple and blue acrylic washes on top of lavender details created using masking fluid. This picture captures sun-baked mounds of scented flowers. The focal point of the warm terracotta-coloured building is surrounded by the complementary colours of violet and yellow and dominates the distant position at the end of the converging lines of lavender.

Crossing the River

50.8 x 40.7cm (20 x 16in)

This tranquil and richly green landscape seems to sum up the beautiful qualities of the countryside. The sheep, the most important element in this composition, suggest a scale. The view leads the eye to this delightful collection of light shapes, their sunlit coats contrasted with the shaded hedge behind. The foreground is understated but equally important as a foil to the dominant animals.

PAINTING SKIES

Skies should not be mere backgrounds to a landscape. The two are inseparable and therefore need to be perfectly related and in harmony with each other.

The whole mood of a landscape will depend on the weather and some understanding of these rapid changes of mood, cloud formation and development will certainly help in painting a convincing scene. Time spent just watching skies is paramount. This will result in a more subtle, sophisticated and in-depth portrayal. You will need to anticipate the possible changes that may occur, especially when painting outside.

Mistakes should be avoided if you prepare by doing a series of brief thumbnail sketches. Their roughness often captures a spontaneous and honest reaction to the sky before you. As in the sketch shown here, I often write down colour notes to help recall that brief moment in time, which is invaluable for future paintings.

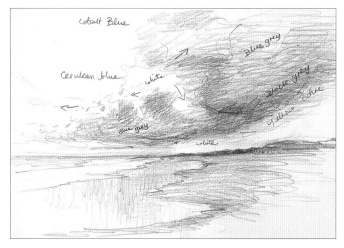

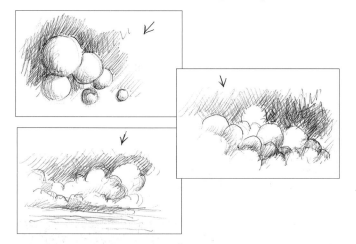

These simplified sketches in ballpoint pen depict the basic forms of clouds with an arrow indicating the direction of sunlight. These can greatly increase your understanding of cloud formations and of how clouds can be separately formed but can also change rapidly into shaded, flowing, fluffy shapes that are continually on the move! The illusion of recession is captured by bunching the clouds and making them smaller towards the horizon, and by altering the tone of the sky, which should be darker in the foreground, with lighter, pastel shades in the distance.

These are stormy clouds of Payne's gray, cobalt blue, white and yellow ochre. The upward thrust of the brush strokes give a rolling movement of the various wave-like clouds, arriving just ahead of the worst of the wind. A rain storm is also present, giving a very dramatic feel.

This develops the drawings into an acrylic painting. With an undercoat of burnt sienna, I placed on cobalt blue with a no. 4 hog hair brush in a criss-cross manner, mixing more white and burnt sienna towards the horizon. This fair-weather study has flat-based clouds and subdued, irregular, fluffy tops of white with added yellow ochre to lift the lights. The soft grey tones of the undersides are cobalt blue and burnt sienna.

Quiet Evening

32.5 x 23cm (12¾ x 9in)

The long, gentle brush stokes are soft and diffused, softening the whole scene. I used alizarin crimson, cobalt blue, cadmium orange, yellow ochre, white and cerulean blue. A drift of smoke wafts across the setting sun and gathering evening mists – which give an atmospheric feel to the landscape below. Cobalt blue was slowly mixed into cerulean with added white, whilst orange, violet (crimson and cobalt) were mixed with white to form apricot wisps around the darker violet clouds and smoke on the horizon area. Care should be taken to match the feel of the sky to the brush strokes used.

Red Sky at Night

33.7 x 23.5cm (13¼ x 9¼in)

This study features effects that are as dramatic as fireworks. Cadmium orange, cadmium yellow, dioxazine violet, burnt sienna, cobalt blue, yellow ochre and white were used. The cloud shapes were washed in with neat yellow and a touch of ochre in a wet-into-wet manner. When dried, I re-wetted their shapes and applied yet another wash on top. This was in dioxazine violet and burnt sienna. The sky was a wintery wash of cobalt blue, but I kept it darker at the top of the picture. Neat orange was placed with a soft no. 6 brush close to the sun and yellow ochre was glazed over after it dried. White outlined the clouds, enhancing them and creating contrast, and finally the sun shape was placed in with a few sparkly rays in white with a tiny touch of yellow ochre.

VARIATIONS ON A THEME

Acrylics are so delightfully versatile and in this chapter we explore exciting ways of painting this countryside scene in several different ways and in different seasons. It is the same tree study alongside a meandering country lane.

Spring
Here we capture the bright green new leaves alongside fresh, yellow daffodils. This is a sketchy approach with free brush strokes and added details of sepia permanent ink. The colours are yellow ochre, burnt sienna, cadmium yellow, white and cerulean blue. A wash of burnt sienna was placed over the initial quick drawing and allowed to dry. I roughly painted in the sky of cerulean blue and white in varying tones. The distant hedges are the same colour but using neater blue with a little green in places. The tree trunk and branches (burnt sienna and green) were painted with a 13mm (½in) hog brush and a rigger. Cadmium yellow and green mixed together formed the new green foliage, the middle-distance field and spring flowers. The path, painted with strong stokes using burnt sienna, formed a darker, shaded foreground. When this was dry, I added details of finer branches, grasses and darker texturing on the tree trunk and fence posts. Glimpses of burnt sienna all over the picture, through the brush stokes, unify the scene.

Summer
This is a celebration of thick and luscious greens, applied with a painting knife. The whole scene is layered with swathes of expressive markings – using several applications with a variety of shapes and sizes of knife. The colours are cerulean blue, Winsor blue, burnt sienna, Hooker's green, white, cadmium yellow and dioxazine purple. The trunk and branches are applied with the side of a knife, whilst the foliage (Hooker's green, cadmium yellow and Winsor blue) is applied by dragging the paint off the top and edges of the knives. The sky could be introduced into the massed leaves of the tree to add more light and banish the density and heaviness if required. The pastel-coloured clouds of white and dioxazine purple are finally added for the light areas and Winsor blue, dioxazine purple and a little burnt sienna for the darker shadows on the trunk, tree foliage, foreground and fence posts.

Autumn Tints

A glorious vibrant season, needing contrasting colours and tones for full effects. Perinone orange, burnt sienna, yellow ochre, white, cerulean blue and dioxazine violet are the colours used. The techniques used are the traditional oil methods. I used dotting and dabbing brush strokes, one on top of another, overlapping colours and intensifying the completed tree with brilliant orange against the cerulean sky blue. A mid-purple middle-distant hedge offsets the light orange path which is covered with dots of burnt sienna and blues for a colourful foreground. Cadmium yellow dots completed the scene with a sunlit feel to the foliage.

Winter

This watercolour style painting used a limited palette of burnt sienna, cobalt blue, white and raw umber. Masking fluid was placed on the snow-laden branches, signpost, foreground cow parsley and fence posts. The main tree was painted in raw umber and cobalt blue, and left to dry. I then used salt sprinkled into a watery raw umber and cobalt blue wash. The path of white, blue and a touch of umber was finally added with a small hog hair brush before rubbing off the dried salt and masking fluid. A watery wash of burnt umber applied with a size 1 rigger was used for the delicate branches and foreground grasses.

35

Constantine Bay

Many factors affect rocky coastlines and shores, controlling the distribution of plants and animal life as well as the wonderfully diverse physical appearance of the rocks. Exposure to the rigours of the ever-changing tides and weather, makes coasts one of the most varied places for the artist to gain inspiration. I adore the sea and will use any excuse to visit my beach hut, bringing along my painting equipment, ready to capture another adventure in nature. The sweeping, reflective surfaces of a tidal bay or beach, a craggy, textured cliff face, a collection of inviting rock pools and a curling wave unfurling along a seashore are all illustrated in this chapter.

This step-by-step demonstration shows Constantine Bay in North Cornwall, where I was brought up. I made a tonal sketch and a quick pen and wash study with important reference and colour notes. The jigsaw-like patterns of the interlocking shapes excited me, and the simplicity of the limited colour palette I wished to use just begged me to have a go!

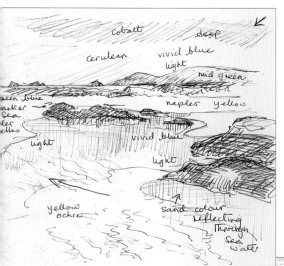

The tonal sketch and the coloured pen and wash study.

Materials

Not 300gsm (140lb) watercolour paper, 40.5 x 30.5cm (16 x 12in)

Colours
  burnt sienna
  yellow ochre
  cerulean blue
  cobalt blue
  titanium white
  dioxazine purple
  Hooker's green
  raw umber
  Naples yellow

13mm (½in) flat brush

No. 2 filbert hog brush

No. 4 round sable brush

Painting knife

Fine sand texture paste

Kitchen paper

Hairdryer

1. Draw the scene. Use a painting knife to spread fine sand texture paste over the foreground and middle rocks. Clean the knife straight away and allow the texture paste to dry or use a hairdryer.

2. Use the 13mm (½in) flat brush to wet the paper all over, then apply a wash of burnt sienna and yellow ochre as an underpainting. Add slightly more burnt sienna in the foreground. Allow to dry.

Tip

When applying an undercoat colour, choose one that will create impact, such as a complementary colour.

3. Begin to paint the sky with a mix of cerulean blue, cobalt blue and white.

4. Add more cerulean blue at the top of the sky for a more intense blue.

5. Paint on white to suggest misty cloud. Continue dabbing on paint, adding texture and interest.

6. Begin to paint the water with the same mix of colours, using vertical strokes of the brush.

7. Add a little dioxazine purple to the mix and continue painting the water with vertical strokes.

8. Paint cobalt blue on the horizon, with horizontal strokes, suggesting the sea in the distance.

9. Mix Hooker's green, burnt sienna and yellow ochre to paint the distant fields. Add raw umber for a browner mix.

10. Use the edge of the brush to create the texture of the rocky area in front of the fields.

11. Paint the rocks in the middle distance and foreground with a mix of burnt sienna, raw umber and yellow ochre.

12. Mix burnt sienna with the sky mix of cerulean blue and cobalt blue, and drag this over the texture paste on the foreground rock.

13. Paint the same dark mix on to the rocks in the middle distance.

Tip

Warm colours used in the foreground help to bring it forwards, whereas cool colours help the distance to recede.

14. Begin to paint the rippled grooves in the foreground sand with a warm mix of burnt sienna and yellow ochre.

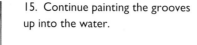

15. Continue painting the grooves up into the water.

16. Change to the no. 2 filbert hog brush and use a mix of Naples yellow and a touch of yellow ochre to paint the lighter parts of the distant rocky area.

17. Use the same colour to paint lighter areas of rippled sand.

18. Darken the foreground area of sand a little with this same mix, so that it is darker than the light area of sand in the middle distance.

19. Highlight the edges of some of the sand ripples with Naples yellow.

20. Drag Naples yellow over the textured surface of the foreground rock.

21. Make a thin mix of dioxazine purple and cobalt blue and glaze this over the foreground water.

22. Paint a wash of dioxazine purple over the foreground water.

23. Dab a little light into the water with a mix of white and cobalt blue.

24. Paint a strong mix of cobalt and cerulean blue to create a vivid colour at the top of the sky.

25. Mix white with dioxazine purple to paint clouds, and rub these in with your finger.

26. Change to a no. 4 round sable brush and paint the crests of waves in the distance with white.

27. Drag a little white across the sand as well.

28. Add a touch of yellow ochre to the white to capture the highlights on the sand ripples.

29. Mix raw umber and burnt sienna to make a dark brown, and paint the dark details on the rocks.

30. Add water to the brown mix and paint details on the distant rocky area.

31. Mix dioxazine purple with raw umber to paint the dark details on the foreground rock.

Tip

Regularly change the water and clean your brushes as a build-up of dry paint will be difficult to clean off and dirty water will affect your painting.

32. Paint the rocks in the far distance with a mix of yellow ochre and dioxazine purple.

33. Use the painting knife with a mix of white and Naples yellow to add light to the ripples in the sand.

34. Still using the painting knife, drag the same mix over the foreground rock to add to the texture.

35. Pick up some of the colour on your finger and drag it down over the water to create reflections.

36. Apply a mix of yellow ochre and burnt sienna with the painting knife in the shaded parts of the sand ripples.

37. Take the no. 2 filbert hog and a mix of white, the sky mix of cobalt and cerulean blue, and yellow ochre, and lighten the most distant part of the water. Add a touch to the foreground water too.

38. Highlight the distant hills with a little yellow ochre.

Tip

At the end of each painting session, thoroughly wash out all brushes and store them upright in a dry container.

Summer Haze

40.6 x 30.5cm (16 x 12in)

This was painted on canvas board. Additional sand was sprinkled into fine texture gel to form the exciting, textured surface and adding sparkle and interest to the undulating sand dunes. Threads of light blue sea water meander towards the distant criss-crossing of the misty racing boat sails.

The Curling Wave

40.6 x 30.5cm (16 x 12in)

This was also painted on canvas board. The palette knife method, using layers of thick paint, was used, applying depth and surface tension in the swirls and layers of paint. This formed the dramatic sky, textured foreground and the whipping up feel of the curling wave. The knife strokes were all done at differing angles, creating surface and structure to each section of this scene. Lighter acrylic paint was then dragged over the foreground, compounding the feeling of beach, seaweed, stones and sand catching the moody light in the sky.

Sunflowers

One of the vistas I love to paint is the panoramic landscape, as illustrated in this demonstration with its atmospheric sense of scale and depth. The distant buildings are from a composite sketch taken from an actual study in Tuscany, and the flowers, also from a sketch, are added in the foreground. The undulating hills need to be simplified and softened into a misty blue to give a sense of vast distance. To avoid the vine-clad countryside being too cluttered and busy, I carefully darkened the tone of each section as it came closer and made the middle distance building resemble a silhouette to give drama and more dominance to the sunflowers in the foreground. The contrasts were now more attractive and direct, with the violet blue shadows behind the sunny yellow of the flower heads.

Although it may seem there is no order to these random flowers, careful sketching out of various compositions were carried out before I decided upon a final solution to this organised chaos!

A reference photograph for the sunflowers.

The composite sketch showing both distant buildings and sunflowers, with an arrow showing the direction of the sunlight.

46

Materials

Not 300gsm (140lb) watercolour paper, 40.5 x 30.5cm (16 x 12in)

Colours:
  cadmium yellow deep
  burnt sienna
  yellow ochre
  titanium white
  cerulean blue
  Naples yellow
  dioxazine purple
  Hooker's green
  cadmium orange
  cobalt blue
  cadmium red
  raw umber

13mm (½in) flat brush

No. 4 flat hog brush

No. 6 sable round brush

Masking fluid and ruling pen

1. Draw the scene. Use a ruling pen and masking fluid to mask the areas where the sunlight catches the flowers.

Tip

Place an arrow at the side of your drawing to remind you of the direction of the sunlight.

2. Paint over the whole paper with a 13mm (½in) flat brush and a mix of cadmium yellow deep and burnt sienna.

3. Paint the foreground with a little more burnt sienna in the mix, then paint the sunflower centres with burnt sienna. Allow to dry.

4. Use the no. 4 flat hog brush and a mix of yellow ochre, burnt sienna and white to paint the sky, leaving parts of the underpainting showing through.

5. Dab on a mix of cerulean blue and white making small, diagonal marks.

6. Leave the right-hand part of the sky with very little blue. Add dabs of Naples yellow into the bluer area.

7. Mix cerulean blue, dioxazine purple and white and paint the far distant hills.

48

8. Add more white and dioxazine purple to the mix and continue building up the hazy, distant hills.

9. Begin to paint the hill in the middle distance, on which the buildings stand, with a darker, bluer mix of the same colours.

10. Paint vertical strokes of this mix in the distance and middle distance, implying the texture of trees and vineyards on the hill.

11. Add a little white to the blue/purple mix to paint fields in front of the hill.

12. Add a little burnt sienna to the mix to paint the silhouette of the buildings on the hill.

13. Add a little more cerulean blue to the mix and continue to paint the buildings with downward strokes.

14. Blend the buildings into the hillside with a bluer mix of the same colours.

15. Mix Hooker's green with a touch of dioxazine purple to paint the trees behind the flowers. These will make a good contrast with the sunflowers. Add more purple to darken the green in places.

16. Make a thin mix of yellow ochre and a little burnt sienna, and glaze this over the distant buildings and forest to lift them a little.

49

17. Create the effect of a heat haze over the far distance with a mix of Naples yellow and white.

18. Mix cadmium yellow deep and Hooker's green to paint the sunlit parts of the middle distance tree tops. Add dabs of the same green in the distance.

20. Lighten the buildings in the middle distance to knock them back further into the distance by painting on a mix of dioxazine purple, cerulean blue and white.

19. Paint some more of the same green to suggest leaves in the foreground. Use a scrubbing motion of the brush.

21. Improve the outline of the buildings using the no. 6 sable round brush and the background sky colour: yellow ochre, burnt sienna and white.

22. Paint a few dark touches of detail on the buildings with a mix of cerulean blue and dioxazine purple.

23. Change to the 13mm (½in) flat brush and freely paint a watered down wash of cadmium yellow deep where the sun catches the sunflowers. Do not paint too thickly, or the paint will dry hard over the masking fluid.

Tip

The drama in a painting comes from contrasts in tone and colour, and this should be most noticeable around the focal point, in this case the sunflowers.

24. Mix burnt sienna and yellow ochre and work this colour into the petals to give a feel of sunlight and shade.

25. Pick up cadmium orange and dab this on to the petals.

26. Mix Hooker's green with dioxazine purple and paint dark areas of greenery, bringing forwards the flower heads by painting negatively around them.

27. Create leaf shapes in the foreground by painting negatively around them with the same dark green.

28. Continue painting green details in the foreground, using the edge and the corner of the brush.

29. Paint the centres of the sunflowers with a mix of raw umber, burnt sienna and a touch of dioxazine purple.

30. Use the no. 6 sable round brush to paint small green details to highlight the edges of the sunflower heads, with a mix of Hooker's green and a little burnt sienna.

31. Make a strong, dark mix of cobalt and cerulean blue and paint accents of this blue among the foliage and round the petals to bring out their brightness.

51

32. Paint the sunlit tops of the trees with a mix of Hooker's green, cadmium yellow deep and white. Allow to dry.

33. Rub off all the masking fluid.

34. Water down cadmium yellow deep and use the no. 4 flat hog brush to paint over the sunlit petals and leaf edges.

35. Paint burnt sienna and yellow ochre on some of the petals to strengthen the shadows. Allow to dry.

36. Glaze a thin mix of dioxazine purple over the hillside for shadow, then add shadow to the flowers with the same glaze.

37. Change to the no. 6 sable round brush to paint around petal shapes and add detail with the dioxazine purple glaze.

38. Mix cadmium orange with white and highlight areas of the petals.

39. Add more highlights with cadmium yellow deep and white.

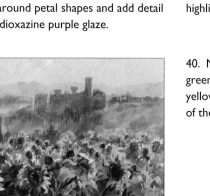

40. Mix a light green from Hooker's green, white and a little cadmium yellow deep and paint the sunlit parts of the sunflower leaves.

41. Make a watered down mix of cerulean blue to paint dark details among the flowers.

42. Mix cadmium orange with a little cadmium red and add bright details to the petals.

43. Add centres to some of the background flowers with raw umber and burnt sienna.

44. Add a touch of cerulean blue to the greenery in the middle distance, and some highlights with cadmium yellow deep.

45. Paint arcs of yellow-green in the dark areas of foliage with a mix of Hooker's green, cadmium yellow deep and white. Add more light to the leaves with the same mix.

46. Use the no. 6 sable round brush with a watered down mix of Naples yellow to knock back the distant building.

47. Finally, darken the building in the far distance with a little dioxazine purple.

Walk in the Vineyard, Tuscany

51 x 40.7cm (20 x 16in)

In complete contrast to the demonstration and in a wet into wet style, this limited palette painting uses cobalt blue, burnt sienna, Hooker's green and yellow, with masking fluid for the light accents. It was mainly painted on site as a demonstration to my students on an Italian art holiday. Again this illustrates the techniques of keeping the distance fluid and simple, and the vines strong and vibrant with the contrasts of tone and colours. The feeling of being drawn into and over the planes of the picture is accentuated by the pathway and lines of vines growing over the middle distant hills. Finally, some of the details were drawn in with sepia water soluble ink.

Cornish Landscape

40.7 x 30.5cm (16 x 12in)

This highly textured surface has glimpses of burnt sienna underpainting showing through it throughout the picture. The strong zigzagging composition of the fields and rugged stone walls in the foreground gives movement and drama to the whole vista. The simplified but colourful foxgloves in front give scale and contrast to the pastel-shaded distance of patchworked fields beyond.

Golden Woodland

Woodlands represent the most diverse collection of plants in any habitat, in any part of the world. This environment contains a blend of textures, colours, wildlife, atmosphere and seasonal changes. There is intense activity all year around, and the glorious trees and other plants create endless opportunities for the painter, as illustrated in this Golden Woodland scene.

Autumn is shimmering, golden and full of contrasts, with many-coloured leaves both adorning the trees and carpeting the ground beneath.

I relied on two sources of reference: firstly a coloured study of my main trees, using a little salt in the preliminary, watery wash, which gave a starry foliage effect. When this was dry, I added thicker paint for the more layered details of the leaves. I also sketched the whole scene in pen and pencil, paying attention to the tonal needs that would be vital to its structure, plus full colour notes.

To capture autumn, you need to paint the first punchy glow in a bright yellow. Adding the forceful, deep violet-brown branches and trunk as a dramatic contrast is a recipe for success!

Left: the colour sketch and below: the pen and pencil sketch with my colour notes.

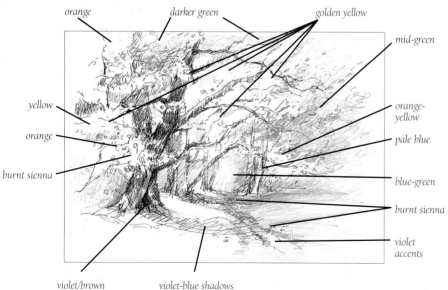

orange   darker green   golden yellow

mid-green

yellow

orange

burnt sienna

orange-yellow

pale blue

blue-green

burnt sienna

violet accents

violet/brown   violet-blue shadows

Materials

Not 300gsm (140lb) watercolour paper, 40.5 x 30.5cm (16 x 12in)

Colours:
  Hooker's green
  dioxazine purple
  cadmium yellow deep
  burnt sienna
  dioxazine purple
  raw umber
  cobalt blue
  cerulean blue
  yellow ochre
  cadmium red
  cadmium orange
  titanium white

Drawing inks in nut brown and canary yellow, ruling pen and distilled water

13mm (½in) flat brush

No. 2 filbert hog brush

1. Draw the scene in pencil.

2. Use the ruling pen to go over parts of the pencil drawing with nut brown ink. When drawing the branches, leaves gaps for foliage. Allow to dry or use a hairdryer to speed up the process.

3. Take the 13mm (½in) flat brush and paint on a wash of canary yellow ink where the golden sunlight shows in the foliage.

4. Water down the ink with a little distilled water and continue painting.

5. While the ink is wet, mix Hooker's green with a little dioxazine purple and paint the foliage at the top of the trees.

6. Add cadmium yellow deep to soften the green and continue to paint foliage lower down.

7. Water down the light green mix and paint strokes across the woodland floor.

8. Still working wet into wet, paint a mix of burnt sienna and cadmium yellow deep on to the ground to suggest fallen leaves.

9. Paint pure burnt sienna in the foliage and on the ground for autumn leaves.

10. Paint the trunk and branches of the left-hand tree where they show through the leaves, with a mix of dioxazine purple and raw umber. Create negative shapes for foliage.

Tip

If in doubt about a colour, try it out on a similar paper before painting.

11. Paint the tree behind the main tree with Hooker's green and a little burnt sienna.

12. Mix cobalt blue and cerulean blue with water and paint the distant trunks, fading up into the foliage.

13. Add cadmium yellow deep into the background.

14. Paint a mix of Hooker's green and cerulean blue into the wet yellow paint.

15. Paint yellow ochre on the ground.

16. Mix a dark brown from dioxazine purple and cerulean blue to paint the darker leaves and the mud in the foreground.

17. Water down the mix to paint shadow on the trees.

18. Paint burnt sienna on the ground for more fallen leaves.

19. Cool down the purple in the foreground and on the main tree trunk by painting on a little cerulean blue.

20. Make a bright mix of cadmium red and cadmium orange and pick it up on your brush. Press the bristles against your finger and then let them go to splatter paint in little drops over the foliage area of the painting.

21. Paint dabs of the same bright mix into the foliage.

60

22. Paint cerulean blue across the woodland path, to help join one side of the painting to the other.

23. Mix dioxazine purple with Hooker's green and splatter paint over the foliage area as before.

24. Paint shaded parts of the foliage with the same mix.

25. Paint more bluey-green in the distance with a mix of cobalt blue and Hooker's green.

26. Splatter dioxazine purple in the foreground, then add dabs of the same mix.

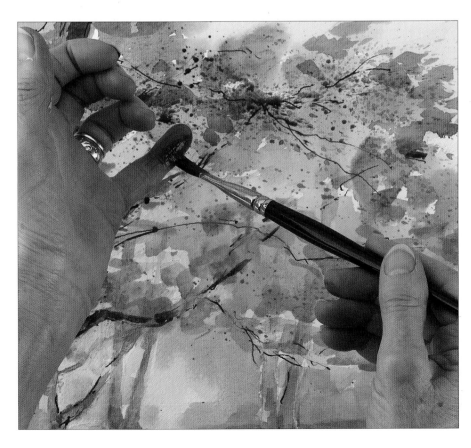

Tip
Spots, flecks and dabs of paint will help to add life to your work, but don't over-do it!

27. Splatter dioxazine purple in the foliage area.

61

28. Dab a dark mix of Hooker's green and dioxazine purple among the foliage to bring out the brightness.

29. Change to the no. 2 filbert hog brush and paint highlights in the foliage with white, cadmium yellow deep and cadmium orange.

30. Paint dabs of light on the ground with the same mix.

31. Use the ruling pen and nut brown ink to reinforce parts of the branches that have been covered by paint.

32. Use the 13mm (½in) brush and cerulean blue with Hooker's green to extend the long branch going across the scene.

33. Splatter a mix of burnt sienna and raw umber across the painting. Allow to dry.

34. Add highlights in various areas of the painting with touches of cadmium yellow deep.

35. Darken the trunks of the background trees with dioxazine purple.

Tip

Using a limited palette of colours gives a cohesive feel to the whole picture, so do not be tempted to add new colours at this stage.

36. Add a thin glaze of cerulean blue and Hooker's green over the bright spot in the background, then splatter burnt sienna over it.

37. Darken the pathway that reaches into the foreground with dioxazine purple.

Winter Wonderland

40.7 x 30.5cm (16 x 12in)

This painting shows a wet into wet approach, using a limited palette of cobalt blue, burnt sienna, yellow ochre, white and dioxazine purple. Masking fluid topped the snow-laden branches, fences and gate structure, giving a beautiful contrast to the darker but misty, atmospheric background. Sepia watercolour ink was added to the branches and some post details, and was used to accentuate the textured tree trunk. To keep the fluidity of acrylics, always wet the paper surface before starting to paint. If it dries, you can re-wet the surface and paint over the first wash.

Sunlit Bluebell Path

45.7 x 35.5cm (18 x 14in)

This open-weaved and freely painted picture uses a variety of widths of hog hair brushes, giving an exciting surface and a lively feel to the layers of bluebells carpeting the dappled undergrowth. The blue-violet tonal shadows contrast with the highlighted trees and flowers in the rich sunlight.

Flowers are not just wholly one colour. As illustrated here, bluebells are not just blue, they consist of a lovely cocktail of pinks, crimsons and darker shadows of blue, plus touches of cobalt and cerulean blues.

The branches also needed altering to create a more flowing and complete composition. Nature, as most artists realise, does not always provide the ideal answer to our artistic needs, but does provide a wonderful guide.

Cows by River

This is an ideal scene for demonstrating acrylic techniques, plus of course the mixing of many different greens! Water creates its own challenges – the tranquil and fluid quality of the movement within the water, the balance of reflection from the objects around the water, and the amount of colour needed to portray a convincing mirrored image. Here, the reflection includes the animals, sky and all the greenery from the plants and trees around. Sometimes I elongate these images, soften them or make them zigzag more gently to place the emphasis on the objects reflected. Water, whatever its guise, adds another marvellous dimension to a painting. I love adding these features to my work, even if it's a rain puddle in the middle of a path to add sparkle to an uninteresting element of the picture. Some painters make reflections a little darker, but I like, on the whole, to reflect the same tones and hues, which creates a good link between the objects above and the water's depths.

The reference photograph.

The finished painting.

66

Materials

Not 300gsm (140lb) watercolour paper,
40.5 x 30.5cm (16 x 12in)

Colours:
 Hooker's green
 cerulean blue
 cadmium yellow deep
 cadmium orange
 burnt sienna
 dioxazine purple
 titanium white
 raw umber
 ultramarine blue

13mm (½in) flat brush

Rigger

Masking fluid and ruling pen

1. Draw the scene. Use masking fluid and a ruling pen to mask out the tops of the cows, the branches and the ripples in the water.

2. Wet the whole paper. Use the 13mm (½in) flat brush with Hooker's green, cerulean blue and cadmium yellow deep to paint the lighter parts of the trees. Bring this down into the water with vertical strokes.

3. Wash and wipe the brush and use it to lift out colour to lighten the distant field.

4. Mix cadmium orange and burnt sienna and drop it into the right-hand tree. Add a little Hooker's green to the mix and a touch of dioxazine purple to paint the reflection.

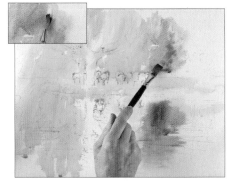

5. Lift out colour from the trees for gaps in the foliage. Drop in burnt sienna and dioxazine purple for darker touches.

6. Paint in a vibrant green mixed from Hooker's green and cadmium yellow deep.

7. Add burnt sienna to brown the mix and paint the mounds at the water's edge. Add more burnt sienna to paint the waterline.

8. Mix cerulean blue and Hooker's green to paint the dark areas of the trees. Soften the edges with clean water while the paint is wet.

9. Paint the reflection of the blue-green down into the water with vertical strokes.

10. Next paint the sky with cerulean blue and a touch of white, bringing the blue down into the gaps between the trees.

12. Paint the trunks of the trees on the right with Hooker's green and dioxazine purple, and paint the tree's reflection with the same colour.

11. Bring the same blue down into the water for the reflections of the sky, using horizontal strokes.

13. Water down burnt sienna to paint the trunks of the central trees and their reflections.

14. Make a stronger mix of burnt sienna and dioxazine purple with a little raw umber for the darker parts of the tree trunks and reflections. Add a few branches.

69

15. Intensify the reddy-brown colour of the right-hand trees and their reflections using burnt sienna and a touch of dioxazine purple.

16. Make a pinky base colour for the cows from watered down burnt sienna. Paint their reflections too.

17. Mix Hooker's green and burnt sienna to darken the light green areas in the water, with horizontal strokes suggesting rippled reflections.

18. Make a thin wash of cerulean blue and paint this on the field near the waterline.

19. Create a dark area in the distance to emphasise the lighter parts of the trees with a mix of cerulean blue and burnt sienna.

20. Mix Hooker's green with cerulean blue and paint this on the waterline and down into the water.

21. Water down a wash of cerulean blue and paint this in the water using horizontal strokes of the brush.

22. Pick up a mix of Hooker's green and cerulean blue, then push the bristles against your finger and release them to splatter little spots of paint over the main tree's foliage.

23. Change to the rigger brush for fine details and use a mix of ultramarine blue and raw umber to paint the black parts of the cows and their reflections.

24. Add slightly more raw umber to make the reflections a little browner. Some of the cows should be painted with burnt sienna.

25. Paint some wispy branches with burnt sienna and raw umber.

26. Mix raw umber and ultramarine blue to paint rippled reflections of the wispy branches.

27. Use dioxazine purple to paint the darkest parts of the trees.

28. Water down the dioxazine purple to paint the reflections.

29. Paint the same purple wash behind the cows, to darken the area before removing the masking fluid.

30. Add more ripples in the water with dioxazine purple.

31. Intensify the dark area on the waterline with the same colour.

32. Dab around the edges of the main trees with the pale dioxazine purple wash, to give the foliage a lacy effect.

71

33. Mix Hooker's green and dioxazine purple and paint darker ripples in the foreground. Allow to dry.

34. Rub off all the masking fluid with clean fingers. Use the 13mm (½in) flat brush to paint Hooker's green and cadmium yellow deep into the main trees and their reflection.

35. Use a mix of pale cerulean blue and white to paint lighter ripples in the water.

36. Add more white to the mix and create highlights with little tapping motions and the end of the brush.

37. Use the same technique and mix to add pale blue ripples just below the waterline.

38. Add more pale blue, painting vertical strokes in the water.

39. Paint a pale wash of burnt sienna over the parts of the cows that were masked, and bring the same colour down into the water.

40. Add shadow to the cows with pale cerulean blue.

Tip
Complementary colours like the pale cerulean blue and burnt sienna create a pleasing effect.

41. Mix cerulean blue with Hooker's green and paint it over the grass near the waterline.

42. Use a rigger brush and ultramarine blue mixed with raw umber to paint dark details on the cows.

43. Add darks to the reflections of the cows in the same way.

44. Widen the reflection of the main trees with ripples of ultramarine blue and raw umber.

46. Highlight the tops of the mounds along the waterline with the same mix.

45. Paint light accents in the water with a mix of white and cadmium yellow deep.

This is an idyllic early morning scene, and the predominant delicate pinks, apricots and soft greens are a glorious background for the sheep and lambs crossing this old brick bridge. The pastel colours are captured in the water, with a glimpse of the sheep, reminding me that there are still fabulous sights that have remained the same throughout the centuries and hopefully will do so for many more.

Oil style painting techniques are ideal for the textural qualities in this scene. I had to take care that the foreground plants did not take attention away from the softer presence of the sheep, as they were the focal point.

Bathing in the River
40.7 x 30.5cm (16 x 12in)

This watery scene adds a watercolour look to the acrylic painting techniques. The sky, water and foreground were placed in with watery washes on top of a wetted surface and allowed to slightly diffuse before I started on the second stage. This was applied with a slightly darker and more detailed wash on top of the dried first stage. The figures, tree branches and foreground were placed in with no. I rigger for more extensive accents in contrast and colour.

Lake Garda

The Italian lakes are a painter's paradise. I have successfully visited these beautiful regions several times with my students. There is a backcloth of undulating and high-peaked mountains, with old churches, castles, houses and cobbled streets clustering like ochre and sienna gems by the lakeside and reflected in iridescent shafts of light in the Mediterranean-blue waters.

The reflections of buildings are a challenge and a delight. Malcesine is a superb example with its pastel-coloured houses of all sizes and shapes topped with rust-coloured pan tile roofs. The dominating feature is the tall castellated tower. I knew this scene would provide inspiration and atmosphere, so I photographed the buildings with my close-up lens for detail and reference. I also did a tonal pen and pencil sketch from the path that leads along the shoreline to the town, so that I would have enough information for the painting. I hope to paint a similar scene but at night, with the contrasts of tone and colours, so one sketch can be interpreted in several ways.

It is also important to remember, when confronted with these imposing, dramatic mountains, that they have a shape, scale and texture characteristic of this region alone.

The reference photograph and the sketch with colour notes.

76

77

Not 300gsm (140lb) watercolour
paper, 40.5 x 30.5cm (16 x 12in)

Colours:
cadmium red
cadmium yellow
titanium white
cerulean blue
ultramarine blue
Hooker's green
burnt sienna
cadmium yellow deep
dioxazine purple
yellow ochre
cadmium orange
raw umber

13mm (½in) flat brush

No. 2 filbert hog brush

No. 6 sable round brush

No. 4 flat hog brush

Rigger

1. Draw the scene.

2. Mix cadmium red, cadmium yellow and a little white. Paint on clean water first with the 13mm (½in) flat brush, then wash on the underpainting, without obscuring the drawing. Leave to dry.

3. Use the no. 2 filbert hog brush to paint the sky and the water with cerulean blue and white.

4. Paint the distant hill with more cerulean blue and less white. Add ultramarine blue.

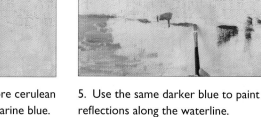

5. Use the same darker blue to paint reflections along the waterline.

6. Mix Hooker's green with burnt sienna to paint the pine trees going up the hill to the castle.

7. Add a little cadmium yellow deep and white to the green and continue painting dabs of greenery and reflections.

8. Use the same mix to paint the hill behind the buildings.

9. Add more white and cerulean blue to the mix to paint the more distant greenery, going round the negative shapes of the buildings.

Tip
When painting buildings, keep everything simple by making horizontal and vertical marks with the corner of a small brush, defining doors, windows and other areas.

10. Add more cerulean blue, Hooker's green and burnt sienna for a strong, dark blue-green and scrub this on to the forested area to create texture.

11. Lighten the hill behind the buildings so that it shows up against the forest, with more cadmium yellow deep and white.

12. Begin to paint colours in the buildings. Mix dioxazine purple, cadmium red and ultramarine blue to paint a shaded building front and its reflection.

13. Add another building front with dioxazine purple and cadmium red.

14. Paint another shaded building front in cerulean blue and bring the colour down into the water.

15. Mix cerulean blue with white and use this to build up the structure of the buildings, painting the shaded sides of the castle and other shaded details.

16. Continue adding details, making the blue mix lighter and darker to vary the effect.

17. Paint other buildings and their reflections with yellow ochre. Add a touch of cadmium orange.

18. Add cadmium yellow deep to the mix to brighten some surfaces further.

19. Change to the no. 6 sable round brush and a pinky-grey mix of burnt sienna, white, cadmium red and cerulean blue to paint roofs and other building details.

20. Add more cadmium red to the grey mix to create warmer details.

21. Mix dioxazine purple, white and yellow ochre to paint more roofs. Add burnt sienna to break up the surfaces.

22. Paint windows on the long building with burnt sienna and cerulean blue.

23. Define the edges of roofs and other details with the same mix.

24. Paint more dark details on the buildings with ultramarine blue.

25. Add dabs of white throughout the painting for highlights.

26. Mix yellow ochre and white and add detail to the castle.

27. Mix burnt sienna, cerulean blue and white and paint the unshaded walls of the castle.

28. Add more cerulean blue and white to grey the mix and paint further shaded details on the buildings.

29. Make a lighter grey by adding more white and cerulean blue and paint the face of the long building and its reflection.

30. Paint shaded details on the castle tower with a mix of yellow ochre and burnt sienna.

31. Mix a bluey-green from Hooker's green and cerulean blue and paint the greenery around the castle.

32. Change to the no. 4 flat hog brush and paint a mix of cerulean blue and white down into the water.

33. Mix cerulean blue and burnt sienna to paint darker reflections.

34. Add downward strokes in the water with a mix of cadmium orange and white, and with cerulean blue and white.

35. Mix cadmium red, cadmium yellow deep and white to paint horizontal strokes in the water, implying the rippled reflections of the pinky-grey roofs.

36. Use the same mix to tone down the darker areas and their reflections.

37. Use the rigger brush and a mix of cerulean blue and raw umber to paint dark details: dots and dashes amidst the jumble of buildings, and texture in the trees.

38. Hint at architectural details in the same way.

39. Paint darker ripples in the water with a mix of Hooker's green and ultramarine blue.

40. Paint lights reflected in the water with a mix of cadmium orange and white.

41. Paint highlights on the buildings with the same mix.

42. Use the no. 4 flat hog brush and a thin mix of cadmium red to drag warm reflections down into the water.

43. Paint around the castle with ultramarine blue to darken the green and define the building's edges.

44. Mix cerulean and white and paint both horizontal and vertical strokes in the water.

45. Paint the misty background with the same pale blue mix to push it further into the distance.

46. Add a little white to the sky, and drag this down into the water.

47. Tone down the brighter oranges in the buildings with white.

48. Paint a shadow under the eaves with cerulean blue. Allow to dry.

49. Use the same blue to paint ripples in the water.

50. Paint the tower and its reflection with a little yellow ochre and white.

51. Finally, add a little cerulean blue to the shadowed side of the tower.

Bellagio – Lake Como

40.7 x 30.5cm (16 x 12in)

The colourful and playful reflections echo the unique village of Bellagio on this lakeside promontory. I used many oil-type techniques over an underpainting of apricot. The glimpses of this colour throughout unite the whole picture and bring it to life. The use of rich mixtures of cadmium yellow and red to form oranges and vivid pinks heighten the impact of the reflections and contrasts. The loose, horizontal brush strokes in the foreground water give it an impressionistic feel, whilst the vertical, tighter strokes on the buildings and church, continued into the mirror image, give depth and interest to the water.

Bradford-upon-Avon Canal

40.7 x 30.5cm (16 x 12in)

Water is a great source of inspiration to me. Here, on my first canal holiday, I produced several watercolour style studies to complete at home. This enchanting, tranquil scene with the strong buildings and blocks of canal boats butted up together caught the very essence of a canal scene for me. Too many details in the reflections would have spoiled the whole effect, but keeping the water simple, with just a little motion in it, caught the moment. I just had to place in the smoke plume from one of the boat's chimney stacks!

Colorado Forest

Painting spectacular scenery is a little like trying to create a beautiful dream, and sometimes we fall short of the masterpiece we had hoped for! When painting mountains, try not to get entangled with small details, but think of the scale, the surrounding distant scenery and the foreground that completes the whole picture. Avoid a harsh feel to the dramatic mountain shape – soften it somewhere, as in the Machu Picchu painting on page 94 with the cloud effect at the base of the mountain – this makes it look more natural.

Hills, mountains or rocks can be textured with special pastes and gels, applied and sculpted with a painting knife. In this demonstration the rocks in the water were textured in this way, and the rocky structure of the distant mountains and the texture of the forest were created with plastic food wrap. You should also try to understand the character and structure of your chosen mountains.

This step-by-step demonstration shows gorgeous Colorado pine-forested hills sweeping down to the water's edge and reflecting mirror-like into the lake. The two sides of the painting contrast with one another in both colour and tone, and the curves of the hills cradle the dominant mountains between them. This see-saw action gives an exciting dynamic to the whole vista, which is a very inviting and challenging exercise.

The sketch.

86

Materials

Not 300gsm (140lb) watercolour paper,
40.5 x 30.5cm (16 x 12in)

Colours:
burnt sienna
cerulean blue
cadmium yellow deep
Hooker's green
raw umber
yellow ochre
titanium white
ultramarine blue

13mm (½in) flat brush

No. 4 flat hog brush

No. 6 sable round brush

Plastic food wrap

Texture paste and painting knife

Kitchen paper

1. Draw the scene.

2. Use the 13mm (½in) flat brush to apply a wash of burnt sienna and cerulean blue over the distant mountains. Vary the wash, painting on more burnt sienna in places.

3. Carefully place a scrunched up piece of food wrap over the wash. The creases will create a craggy texture. Move the food wrap around to change the direction of the creases.

4. You can lift the food wrap and add more paint underneath it if you need to darken the effect in places. Leave until completely dry.

5. Wet the area of the right-hand hillside and paint on the same grey, then cadmium yellow deep, wet into wet. Add Hooker's green to the yellow and paint on this bright green, still working wet into wet.

6. Add food wrap to this area as before.

7. While the washes under the food wrap dry, apply texture paste to the rocks in the water with the painting knife. Allow to dry.

8. Make sure the wash on the distant mountains is dry, and carefully remove the food wrap to reveal the textured effect.

Tip

You might prefer to paint with your drawing board at a slight angle, but when you apply cling film, make sure you leave the painting to dry flat, so the wash does not run.

9. Use the no. 4 flat hog brush to paint the highlights in the left-hand hillside, and some reflections, with cadmium yellow deep. Then mix raw umber and cerulean blue and begin to paint the darker areas.

10. Add a little more cerulean blue to deepen the brown, then more still to paint the pines in the middle distance.

11. Mix raw umber and burnt sienna for a dark rock colour and dab it on to create texture.

12. Add yellow ochre to the brown mix and paint more rocks at the base of the left-hand forested hillside.

13. Paint down into the tree area with raw umber and burnt sienna.

14. Mix cerulean blue and white and paint the top part of the sky, then soften the edges with clean water and dab out with kitchen paper to create the effect of clouds over the mountains.

15. Paint trees and their reflections with Hooker's green and yellow ochre.

16. Add dabs of cadmium yellow deep wet into wet in the trees and reflections.

17. Vary the green mix and continue adding trees and reflections.

18. Mix raw umber and burnt sienna and paint dark, rippled reflections with horizontal strokes.

19. Use cadmium yellow deep to paint bright reflections on the right.

20. Mix burnt sienna with the yellow and paint reflections near the waterline.

21. Add Hooker's green to the mix and bring it down into the water with vertical strokes to reflect the right-hand hillside.

22. Mix raw umber and burnt sienna and add horizontal strokes for dark reflections along the waterline.

23. Add texture to the left-hand forested area with a mix of Hooker's green and burnt sienna.

Tip
Move over the whole picture, rather than completing one area at a time, as this will help to balance the painting well.

24. Paint reflections in the lake with the same mix and a little cerulean blue.

25. Paint a little sky reflection in the water with cerulean blue mixed with white.

26. Remove the food wrap from the right-hand hillside, making sure the paint is completely dry. Paint dabs of yellow ochre on the rocks on the left-hand hillside.

27. Mix Hooker's green with a touch of burnt sienna and paint the trees coming down the right-hand hillside. Change to the no. 6 sable round brush and paint more details of trees.

28. Continue painting trees and their reflections.

29. Paint dark details among the trees with a mix of Hooker's green and cerulean blue.

30. Add burnt sienna to the mix and continue painting details in the trees. Paint the textured rocks in the foreground with yellow ochre, then add darker details with raw umber and burnt sienna.

31. Mix a pale yellow from white and cadmium yellow deep and paint highlights in the trees and trunks.

91

32. Highlight the tops of the rocks in the lake with yellow ochre and white.

33. Work on rippled reflections in the water, with short horizontal strokes of the brush and a mix of burnt sienna and cadmium yellow deep.

34. Paint the reflection of the distant mountains with a grey mix of cerulean blue, burnt sienna and white.

35. Use the same grey mix to add shade to the mountains.

36. Add shadow to the forested area with cerulean blue.

37. Mix burnt sienna with cerulean blue and paint the reflection of the little ridge of trees on the right.

38. Touch in highlights among the trees and rippled reflections with cadmium yellow deep and white.

Tip
Keep massed trees assorted shapes and sizes to give them a more natural feel.

39. Imply deep shadows in the trees with ultramarine blue.

40. Paint light ripples in the water with a mix of white and cerulean blue.

41. Apply streaks of cerulean blue to darken the rocks in the middle distance, and to darken the waterline and add reflections.

42. Intensify the end tree and some others by adding touches of cerulean blue.

43. Paint streaks of cerulean blue in the foreground to reflect the intense blue at the top of the sky.

44. Finally, highlight the trees on the left of the painting with cadmium yellow deep.

Malvern Ridgeway
40.7 x 30.5cm (16 x 12in)

A truly extraordinary view, inviting the viewer across these undulating hills to the blue patchwork of fields and landscape beyond. The hillsides are well trodden and encircled by pathways that lead the eye across the picture.

Golden gorse and purple thistles encrust the grass-filled foreground – this close-up gives more depth to the whole scene. This area was primarily palette-knifed in with white acrylic paint for the weeds and grasses and allowed to dry. Washes were applied on top, forming exciting ridges and patterns for the texturing of the foliage and flowers. This painting was completed in an oil manner and captures everything I adore about the English countryside.

Opposite
Machu Picchu
40.7 x 30.5cm (16 x 12in)

This Lost City of the Incas rises miraculously out of the lush cloud forest, framed by the steep, protective surrounding mountains. It is one of the wonders of the ancient world. After simply wondering and viewing the ruins at different levels, I decided upon this viewpoint. Sometimes this scene can be lost in clouds for hours, but as they fortunately lifted, I captured this awesome view as the large cloud swirled and softened the ruins below. I smudged in its shape with wetted white acrylic paint on my fingertips, diffusing it into ultramarine blue for the shade underneath. I painted in the background in two wet into wet stages: one for the distant, majestic mountains and sky, and when that was dry, the second for the massive shape of Machu Picchu. The ruined steps were sculpted in with the side of my palette knife and then highlighted with ochre and white with the tip of my knife for the finer details.

INDEX

additives 6, 8, 26–27
  food wrap 6, 10, 11, 26, 27, 86, 88, 91
  PVA glue 26, 27
  salt 6, 26, 35, 56
  texture paste/gel 6, 9, 10, 11, 26, 38,
  39, 44, 86, 88
atmosphere 12, 13, 16, 30, 56

beach 36, 45
boat 14, 44, 85
brushes 8, 9, 25, 42, 43, 65
building 21, 31, 46, 49, 50, 53, 76, 78,
  79, 80, 81, 82, 83, 84, 85

cloud 32, 33, 38, 41, 86, 89, 95
complementary colours 31, 72
composition 13, 16, 20–21, 29, 30, 31,
  46, 55, 65
  focal point 14, 20, 21, 28, 30, 31,
  50, 74
cows 66, 68, 70, 71, 72, 73

field 13, 17, 29, 30, 31, 34, 39, 49, 55,
  68, 70, 95
flower 13, 27, 29, 34, 46, 48, 49, 51,
  52, 53, 65, 95
  bluebell 12, 13, 65
  sunflowers 46–53
foliage 9, 10, 24, 26, 28, 34, 35, 51, 53,
  56, 58, 59, 60, 61, 62, 68, 70, 71, 95
forest 49, 79, 86–93, 95

grass(es) 23, 29, 34, 35, 73, 95

highlight 40, 42, 51, 52, 53, 62, 63, 72,
  73, 80, 82, 89, 91, 92, 93
horizon 32, 33, 39

ink 6, 19, 34, 54, 58, 62, 64

knives 8, 9, 24, 34

lake 6, 20, 21, 76–83, 84, 86, 90
landscape 6, 12, 14, 15, 16, 22, 23, 28,
  31, 32, 33, 46, 95

mountain 6, 29, 76, 86, 88, 89, 92

oil 6, 9, 22, 24, 35, 74, 84, 95

perspective 18, 28
photograph 12, 14, 15, 21, 28, 29, 30,
  46, 76

reflection 14, 19, 43, 66, 68, 69, 70, 71,
  72, 73, 76, 78, 79, 81, 82, 84, 85, 89,
  90, 91, 92, 93
river 17, 20, 31, 66–73, 74
rock 26, 36, 38, 39, 40, 42, 43, 86, 88,
  89, 91, 92, 93

sand 39, 40, 42, 43, 44, 45
sea 14, 26, 36, 39, 44
  wave 36, 41, 45
shadow 14, 17, 18, 23, 28, 34, 46, 52,
  60, 65, 83, 92
sketch(ing) 12, 13, 14, 16, 18, 19, 21,
  28, 30, 32, 36, 46, 56, 76, 86
sky/skies 20, 32–33, 34, 39, 41, 45, 48,
  50, 66, 69, 74, 78, 83, 89, 90, 93, 95

techniques
  collage 6, 27
  glaze/glazing 6, 23, 40, 49, 52, 63
  impasto 10, 24
  masking fluid 11, 22, 31, 35, 48, 50,
  52, 54, 64, 68, 71, 72

pen and wash 11, 36
scratching out 9, 23, 25
scumbling 24
splatter(ing) 23, 60, 61, 62, 63, 70
sponging 23
underpainting 13, 18, 38, 48, 55,
  78, 84
wash(es) 6, 9, 11, 22, 26, 27, 31, 33,
  34, 35, 38, 41, 50, 56, 70, 71, 72, 74,
  78, 88, 95
wet into wet 6, 22, 33, 54, 59, 64, 88,
  89, 95
texture 13, 26, 27, 38, 39, 43, 49, 56,
  76, 79, 82, 86, 88, 89, 90
tone 12, 14, 17, 18–19, 29, 30, 32, 34,
  35, 50, 54, 66, 76, 86
tree 14, 15, 17, 19, 23, 24, 29, 30, 34,
  35, 49, 50, 52, 56, 58, 59, 60, 63, 64,
  65, 66, 68, 69, 70, 71, 72, 73, 74, 78,
  82, 89, 91, 92, 93

watercolour 6, 9, 10, 12, 22, 35, 38, 48,
  58, 68, 74, 78, 85, 88

Spring Lane

40.7 x 30.5cm (16 x 12in)